REAL LIFE VAMPIRES

BLOODSUCKING BIRDS

BY CHRISTINE HONDERS

Gareth Stevens
PUBLISHING

Please visit our website, www.garethstevens.com. For a free color catalog of all our high-quality books, call toll free 1-800-542-2595 or fax 1-877-542-2596.

Cataloging-in-Publication Data

Honders, Christine.
Bloodsucking birds / by Christine Honders.
p. cm. — (Real-life vampires)
Includes index.
ISBN 978-1-4824-3939-7 (pbk.)
ISBN 978-1-4824-3940-3 (6 pack)
ISBN 978-1-4824-3941-0 (library binding)
1. Birds — Juvenile literature. 2. Rare birds — Juvenile literature. 3. Birds — Galapagos Islands — Juvenile literature. I. Honders, Christine. II. Title.
QL676.2 H66 2016
598—d23

First Edition

Published in 2016 by
Gareth Stevens Publishing
111 East 14th Street, Suite 349
New York, NY 10003

Designer: Katelyn E. Reynolds
Editor: Kristen Nelson

Photo credits: Cover, pp. 1, 17 Stuart G Porter/Shutterstock.com; cover, pp. 1–24 (background art) happykanppy/Shutterstock.com; pp. 5 (image), 11 Mark Jones Roving Tortoise Photos/Oxford Scientific/Getty Images; p. 5 (map) vasosh/Shutterstock.com; pp. 7, 15 Tui De Roy/Minden Pictures/Getty Images; p. 9 Paul van den Berg/Shutterstock.com; p. 13 Endless Traveller/Shutterstock.com; p. 19 Villiers Steyn/Shutterstock.com; p. 21 (bird silhouette) Fotonium/Shutterstock.com.

Printed in the United States of America

CPSIA compliance information: Batch #CW16GS: For further information contact Gareth Stevens, New York, New York at 1-800-542-2595.

CONTENTS

Bloodsucking Birds. 4

Vampire Finches. 6

Hood Mockingbirds 8

Why Blood? 10

The Galapagos Islands 12

Only the Strong Survive 14

Oxpeckers 16

Not So Helpful 18

Endangered! 20

Glossary. 22

For More Information 23

Index 24

Words in the glossary appear in **bold** type
the first time they are used in the text.

BLOODSUCKING BIRDS

Birds are interesting animals that come in different shapes, sizes, and colors. Some birds, like eagles, fly high in the sky, and some, like penguins, can't fly at all. They may eat seeds, fish, nuts, insects, worms, or even mice!

A few kinds of birds have an unusual part to their **diet**. In the Pacific Ocean, 600 miles (966 km) off the coast of South America on the Galapagos Islands, there are birds that drink blood! Prepare to meet some real-life vampires!

This is a vampire finch. It's named for a made-up monster called a vampire that's said to drink people's blood.

North America

Galapagos Islands

South America

VAMPIRE FINCHES

Vampire finches look much like other finches that don't drink blood except for one thing: they have very sharp beaks that are perfect for drawing blood.

It's believed that in the past, vampire finches would peck fleas and ticks out of the tail feathers of seabirds. Their beaks would break the seabirds' skin and cause them to bleed. The vampire finches started drinking the blood! The seabirds became so used to the finches pecking them that they never tried to get away.

FACT BITE

Vampire finches are part of a larger group of birds called ground finches. The males have mostly black feathers, and the females are gray with brown streaks.

Sometimes vampire finches even take turns feasting on the same seabird.

HOOD MOCKINGBIRDS

Most mockingbirds are known for their beautiful songs. Hood mockingbirds are known for having a taste for blood! They also enjoy dining on seabird eggs and dead animals. Yuck!

Hood mockingbirds will drink blood from the wounds of sea lions, but they'll also try to get at cuts on people's legs! They're not afraid of people at all. In fact, sometimes they'll land on a person's head to see if they have any food.

Hood mockingbirds have gray and brown feathers with a white underside. They also have long, thin beaks useful for breaking into seabirds' eggs.

FACT BITE
Hood mockingbirds have been known to chase people and try to steal their water by pecking at water bottles!

WHY BLOOD?

Why do these birds drink blood? They commonly eat the seeds and insects other birds do. However, the Galapagos Islands are very dry, and sometimes food is hard to find. Long ago, these birds found that blood drawn from pecking at other animals was a good addition to their diet, especially when food was **scarce**. Furthermore, blood is very **nutritious**!

Over time, these birds have found a way to survive in their **habitat**—even if it's a little creepy to us!

FACT BITE

A change in an animal's **behavior** or body that makes it better suited to its habitat is called an adaptation.

THE GALAPAGOS ISLANDS

The hood mockingbird and the vampire finch live on the Galapagos Islands and nowhere else. It may seem strange that two different bloodsucking birds come from the same place.

The islands were formed about 700,000 to 5 million years ago in the middle of the ocean. No plants or animals lived there. Over time, animals found their way to the islands by swimming or flying. Plant seeds were blown in by the wind and began to grow.

FACT BITE

The Galapagos Islands get little rainfall, and the air and water aren't very warm.

There are 13 large islands and 7 small islands that make up the Galapagos Islands.

ONLY THE STRONG SURVIVE

There was very little food on these dry, rocky islands, so the first animals fought for every bite. The animals that were most successful passed their **characteristics** on to their babies when they **reproduced**.

Charles Darwin, a **naturalist**, went to the islands in 1835 and discovered 13 different kinds of finches. Even though they came from the same **ancestors**, each had a different beak. Finches that ate large nuts had strong beaks, finches that ate insects had skinny beaks, and the bloodsucking finches had sharp beaks.

At some point long ago, finches with sharp beaks discovered
a filling meal of blood—and the behavior was passed on!

FACT BITE

The different beaks of
the finches helped Darwin to come up
with his theory of **evolution**. A theory
is an idea that explains something and
is formed from careful study of facts.

OXPECKERS

There's another bloodsucking bird that lives in Africa. Sometimes called a tickbird, red-billed oxpeckers have a mostly gray-brown body with a pale yellow underside. You know you've spotted one when you see the yellow circle around its eye and a short red bill. They're fairly small, only growing to about 9 inches (23 cm) long.

The oxpecker is commonly found sitting on big African **mammals** such as oxen, impalas, and rhinos. It's their blood the oxpeckers drink!

With its bright red beak, the red-billed oxpecker already looks like it drinks blood!

NOT SO HELPFUL

Scientists once thought oxpeckers were a big help to other animals. When oxpeckers hang out on African mammals, they eat ticks off the mammals' ears, necks, and heads. Ticks suck the larger animal's blood and can give animals illnesses, so the oxpeckers are helping them, right? Wrong!

Oxpeckers actually wait until the tick is full of blood and then eat it. The harm to the mammal is already done. Oxpeckers also make the tick bites bigger so they can drink more blood!

FACT BITE
Because of the oxpecker,
it takes some mammals' wounds
a long time to heal.

ENDANGERED!

As scary as these birds may seem, we're much more dangerous to them than they are to us. Human activities like hunting, overfishing, and even too many visitors can be harmful to them. Since bloodsucking birds live in very few places around the world, it's important to keep them safe.

Vampire finches are endangered, which means there are so few of them that soon they may not exist at all! Hood mockingbirds aren't endangered yet, but it's believed there are only about 2,500 left on the Galapagos Islands.

WHAT YOU DON'T KNOW ABOUT BLOODSUCKING BIRDS

- Sometimes vampire finches get so hungry they drink the blood of their own dead.

- Vampire finches steal eggs from nests and then work to break their shells as a team so they can all eat together.

- Vampires finches don't just pick on adult seabirds. They'll go right up to seabird nests and peck at the baby chicks until they bleed!

- Vampire birds live on two islands in the Galapagos called Darwin Island and Wolf Island. Hood mockingbirds live on Española Island.

- Vampire birds have been known to eat what other animals throw up.

- Hood mockingbirds have close families and work together caring for their young.

- Oxpeckers eat whatever they can get off the skin of bigger animals, like dead skin, sweat, or tears.

GLOSSARY

ancestor: one who comes before others in a family

behavior: the way an animal acts

characteristic: a quality that makes something different from other things

diet: what an animal usually eats

evolution: the process of animals and plants slowly changing into new forms over thousands of years

habitat: the place where an animal lives

mammal: a warm-blooded animal that has a backbone and hair, breathes air, and feeds milk to its young

naturalist: someone who studies plants and animals as they live in nature

nutritious: containing things needed to grow and stay alive

reproduce: when an animal creates another creature just like itself

scarce: not plentiful

FOR MORE INFORMATION

Books

Ashby, Ruth. *Young Charles Darwin and the Voyage of the Beagle*. Atlanta, GA: Peachtree, 2009

Chin, Jason. *Island: A Story of the Galapagos*. New York, NY: Roaring Brook Press, 2012.

Websites

Blood-Eating Animals
www.nwf.org/Kids/Ranger-Rick/Animals/Mixture-of-Species/Blood-Eating-Animals.aspx
Learn about other bloodsucking animals.

Vampire Birds
toughlittlebirds.com/2014/10/29/vampire-birds/
See pictures of lots of vampire birds.

Vampire Finches
www.animalplanet.com/tv-shows/animal-planet-presents/videos/top-10-bloodsuckers-vampire-finches/
Watch a video of vampire finches.

INDEX

adaptation 11

Africa 16, 18

African mammals 16, 18

beaks 6, 9, 14, 15

behavior 11, 15

characteristics 14

Darwin, Charles 14, 15

diet 4, 10

eggs 8, 9, 11, 21

evolution 15

Galapagos Islands 4, 10, 12, 13, 20, 21

ground finches 6

habitat 10, 11

hood mockingbirds 8, 9, 11, 12, 20, 21

insects 4, 10, 14

red-billed oxpeckers 16, 17, 18, 19, 21

seabirds 6, 7, 8, 9, 11, 21

sea lions 8

seeds 4, 10, 12

ticks 6, 18

vampire finches 5, 6, 7, 11, 12, 20, 21